The Magical World of Twigshire

A Feel Good Book for All Ages

by Judi Light

Publisher
Light Touch Art™
Venice, Florida

 ™

Light Touch Art™
Venice, FL 34292

ISBN-10: 0615717896

ISBN-13 978-0-615-71789-0

Library of Congress Control Number: 2012952111

Text design by Judi Light & Eric Barnes
This book was electronically typeset in Comic Sans. Cover and title page are in Zapfino.

Published by Light Touch Art, Venice, Florida, USA

Giclée prints provided by Quicksilver Photo Lab, Bellingham, WA

Printing and Binding provided by CreateSpace, an Amazon company.

DEDICATION

This book is dedicated to Eric and Kiera.

Thank you, Eric, for all your hard work and persistence.

Thank you, Kiera, for your lifetime of belief in my art.

Thank you both for your ongoing love and support.

I love and appreciate you both very much.

HARRY TAKES FIVE

Harry has an important job working for a VERY big company.

Each day his assignment is to go out and count as many flowers as he can and report back to his boss, Mother Nature.

She told him that no flower is too small and no petal is too droopy, so count them ALL.

Whew! That's a LOT of buzzing about and it can be stressful sorting things out and trying to keep the numbers correct. (He is not supposed to count weeds.. that job belongs to someone else.)

Harry loves his job, is never bored and is willing to work from dawn to dusk.

Once in a while though he takes a bit of a rest.. and today is one of those days.

He remembered something MN (Mother Nature) said to him when he was given the job so long ago:

"When you fly here and there and it takes all day to do it,

take a break, slow it down, relax, my friend.

Create the time, eat a bagel, have a chat with a pal

'Cause ONLY WORKING makes you blue in the end.

Enjoy the sky and the air, breathe the perfume in your day,

Linger long and take your time to walk those miles.

When it's all said and done and everything's been counted

What's important is the number of your smiles."

judi/2012

NEW BEGINNINGS

Wally had been doing the same things for as long as he could remember. He woke up each day at the same time, thought the same thoughts and always ate the same cereal. Each day. Every day.

This morning he awoke and in a flash decided he'd change. He'd go on a journey, a new adventure, down a new path. Why he'd seen one - a new path - out of the corner of his eye, just the other day when he was walking with his best friend, Gilda the Turtle.

So off they went, just like that! (Sometimes it happens this way you know....Big Changes often come from Sudden New Ideas.) He was very excited and just a teeny bit nervous about the adventure ... so he made up this song to sing along the way, that seemed to help make things not so scary:

"I have the things I need the most and I left all the this and the that,
I don't need gray thoughts, or all my old junk, but I do need to bring my bright hat.
And I don't need the dusty old trunk full of cobwebs, that get in my thoughts and my eyes.
So I'll take my nice chair, my cushion and grapes, and turn my face up to new skies.
If I get a bit scared, don't know what to do, I know I don't need to be glum.
It's a new day, a new journey, it's all here inside me, besides, I have Gilda, my Chum."

6

CEDRIC - FEELING TALL

Cedric had always been rather on the diminutive (that means small-ish) side of life. Things were always either out of reach (too high up) or sounded like this: "Now Cedric.. you know only BIG people can do that."

So every morning, Cedric would step up onto his Support Stool (Hank) ... up on his tip toes ... smile ... breathe deeply ... and then ... he would ... FEEL TALL!.

And the most amazing thing happened each and every time Cedric did this ... He felt good. He felt in charge ... and he KNEW he would succeed as the new Judge at the Mushroom and Whipped Cream Cake eating contest in the spring.

He just KNEW it!

"I'm big in my head, I'm tall in my mind
I'm a Prince, I'm a King, I'm a hero!

If I think that I'm small, if I think I'm too short
That's the wrong way to think, it's a zero!

I'm grand in my eyes and I'm all I can be
I think it, I know it, I AM
I have a big goal, a tall order to fill,
I wish it, I want it, SHAZAM!"

It's GOOD TO FEEL TALL .... THOUGHT CEDRIC

SOPHIE'S SPA DAY

Sophie is obviously an Elfalump, which of course you all knew.

What you might not realize is that whilst her day-to-day lifestyle is not particularly taxing, it does get very messy and muddy trompsing through the marshes and banks of Frog Swallow Lake and the Pondering Pond.

Pigs hunt for truffles, Elfalumps hunt for snuffles, which are much harder to find and require a lot of digging. (Elfalumps sense Snuffles using the little antennae thingies on the tops of their heads). Once found though, snuffles are delicious mixed with spinach and asparagus, finished with a small dish of thistle-down parfait. (Sophie has a Snuffle delivery business providing them to the Rowdy Toad.)

Once in a while Sophie treats herself to a pedicure and a Fish Mist Facial seated under the sun lamp at Zelda's Hot Spot Spa. The Spa is a recent addition to the town of Twigshire and is doing quite a nice steady business.

There is a plaque on the wall of the Spa to remind us all to be good to ourselves. It reads:

"I'm worth a lot, I'm worth the time,
I'm worth some love and care,
So now and then I'll make the time
To be treated with some flair.

Paint my tootsies and cut my tresses,
Take me shopping for three new dresses.
I'm worth a lot, I'm worth the time
I'm worth some love and care."

FIONA'S FIRST BEATLES EXPERIENCE

Fiona is a bustling Twigshire citizen, whose job it is to conduct the talent shows for the Rowdy Toad during the busy summer months.

She is also taking singing AND dancing lessons at the Twigshire Community Center, is in charge of the Maypole Festival in the Spring and is auditioning local talent for the event.

Someone told her about a great new music sound....by some bugs... the Beatles or.. potato Bugs.. or some such...

(I think it was the Beatles.)

Fiona is excited to hear the audition, even though there is only one band member auditioning...(it would appear that he is very very good and she couldn't help but break out into her favorite clog dance while this little guy was singing his heart out:

" Ya gotta dance, dance, dance
Don't step on the ants, ants, ants

Ya gotta wiggle what you can jiggle
Even if it makes ya giggle, giggle, giggle

"Yeh, yeh yeh, yehhhhhhhhh"

(I'm thinking he writes his own lyrics though and has a day job somewhere.)

SCRUM & ANGELO

I remember in school, Science Class perhaps, being taught some blather about how and why leaves change color in the fall. Something about oxygen levels, and cold weather and such.

The fact of the matter is ... at least in Twigshire, out past the Pondering Pond, why even stretching as far north and west as Frog Swallow Lake ... the leaves turn color the way that they have done for eons.

Angelo and his sturdy workmate Scrum, go hither and thither with their Never Ending Burnishing Brush ... and, with a gentle flourish of the bristles, they Majickly create the brilliant colors of fall. But, of course, you all knew that. Silly me.

"The summer is gone and the leaves are green, now they need to be gold and red,
So I ask my pal Scrum to kneel down low and I climb on top of his head.
With a flick of my brush and some Majick Paint, with a stroke of my arm that's bold,
In the blink of an eye, just a second of time, and "POOF!" all the leaves are now gold."

LIMP IMP SOUP

Limp Imp Soup is a specialty at the Rowdy Toad. Chef Frederich created the recipe and kept it secret for hundreds of years, and has only just released it for the general public.

Low Calorie Limp Imp (and Posy) Soup Recipe

This soup is nutritious and packed with everything one would expect from a majick, loveable, naughty bit of imp!

1 medium or 2 small Imps ... with or without swim cap

5 cups of posy petals (the brighter the color the better)

25 gallons of fresh rain water.

A dash of chickweed salt

and ground pollen pepper to taste.

Heat water over very low heat. (The Imp gets limp from a long leisurely soak.) Gradually add the petals and seasonings. Cooking time: 37 hours. (You will know the soup is done when the Imp starts to snore.) Remove imp and lay him out to dry on a nice blanket. (You can reuse him over and over ... sort of like a tea bag ... he doesn't mind at all.) Serve the soup up with a big slice of freshly baked Bullrush Bread.

Enjoy!

FLYING HIGH

You know there are days when things aren't quite right,
When I'm just a bit grey, in a mood.
I know it's not me and I know it won't last
But still, I do tend to brood.

And then I remember,
(Oh silly ol' me)
It's like flipping a switch in the night!
I just choose a thought that's a happier one
and Drizelda and I take to flight!

Up up and away, above chimneys and trees,
Far up past the clouds and the grey,
Drizelda and I swoop and glide with the birds,
It's now a much happier day.

WILMA'S DAY OFF

Work, Work, Work. Wilma has been a very busy gal typing up the invitations for the "Spring Festival of Events at The Rowdy Toad, Twigshire Village Green and Pondering Pond Bowling Alley".

(It had been mentioned that the title was a tad too lengthy, but that sent Wilma into a tizzy!)

Lots to do and only 8 fingers to do it!

The Shire Mayor surprised Wilma with a day off with pay, lunch and total admiration from everyone.

So far so good....her strawberry frappé is excellent, the men doting...and her shoes...well..what can one say? Not only are they designer.. but they were on SALE!

MANNY BABA & ODETTE

Twigshire is a growing community. Obviously, word is spreading that it is a happening Shire.
(I know that the Posy and Limp Imp soup served at the Rowdy Toad is getting quite the reputation and folks are coming from miles west of the Pondering Pond to get some.)

Manny Baba has made quite the journey on his ostrich, Odette, through sand dunes, oil fields and rug sales, just to arrive in time for the Maypole event in the spring. And to taste some of the famous Limp Imp Soup at the Rowdy Toad.

Odette, who has been on this trip for months, is really looking forward to a good leg wax and facial.

To make the long road trip seem to go much faster Odette created this word game for she and Manny to play along the way. Odette would ask the question and Manny had to come up with an answer right away.

What is bigger than the moon?
This crazy, gritty, big sand dune!

What is wider than this sky?
My Grandma's homemade pecan pie!

When will we ever get to town?
I don't know, don't make me frown.

I know how to make you laugh,
Just think about a nice hot bath!

Odette told me they played this game pretty much all the way from Rugs Are Us in Fez Town, until they arrived in Twigshire.

FROG SWALLOW LAKE FLYING FISH SOCIETY

Mz. Emelda Flapjacket, the local Twigshire Historian and
Librarian, is also the proud founder of the
Frog Swallow Lake Flying Fish Society.

Founded umpteen years ago, membership is rather slim, but Ferb,
an avid photographer of "All Things Wonderful, Unusual and
Nifty", has just joined up and Emelda is taking him on his
very first Field Trip.

Over time, Mz. Flapjacket has observed much rare behavior
amongst the fish, one of them being that some delight in wearing
ribbons on Wednesdays. And, fortunately, Ferb was there to
witness and photograph this very thing.

Emelda was just now mentioning to Ferb:

"You can read about these fishies in some very old rare books.
I've told some folks about them, but they wouldn't come and look.

They all thought I was loopy and that none of it was real,
But now that you are here, you can see and touch and feel.

Are they all not beautiful, so friendly, shy, yet witty?
And the one who has the ribbon is exceptionally pretty."

Look for Ferb's photos on the bulletin board in the Library.

APPRECIATION

Mr. Bumberdorn made up his mind that it was high time. It seemed nobody else had even given it so much as a passing thought over these many months. So he just went ahead on his own... and did it.

He put on his "Special Occasion With The Fancy Flowers and Extra Starch In The Tails Coat" (which he hadn't worn before because he hadn't had any Special Occasions to attend), laced up his Extra Sturdy Walking Boots and headed off to the Flitter Bug Fields.

Nobody went with him to take notes and report it in the Weekly Shire Newspaper. Why nobody even saw him leave the Rowdy Toad where he'd eaten lunch.

When he finally found the perfect spot, he sat and waited...and waited...and waited. Suddenly, he saw a glimmering flitter and there he was...A Flitter Bug!

The wee chap sat down opposite Mr. Bumberdorn and smiled "hello". And Mr. Bumberdorn said:

"Well now, wee chap, it's been a long while
since we've told you and yours how we feel.
I came all this way 'cause I wanted to say,
(even though some don't think that you're real)

I appreciate you and all that you do, for me
and the folks in the town.
It's not said enough, no, it's not and that's true,
but regardless you don't let us down.

You just keep on shining and giving us light,
with cheer and such wonderful spark.
Many thanks for your work, done with heart and much love,
But for you, we'd be in the dark."

THE TRAVELER AND THE IBIS

"How do you do?"
Said the man to the Ibis
As they met one another on the road.
(An Ibis is a bird with a long orange beak,
That likes to eat bugs and toads.)

"I'm grand and thank you",
He replied to the man, "And where are you headed this day?"
"I'm not quite sure" the chubby bloke smiled,
"Do you think you can show me the way?"

The odd looking bird pointed south, north, east, west
And also, just whence it might rain,
Then suggested the bloke flag a cab, ride a bus
Or even, if flush, take the train.

The fine looking chap hemmed and hahhed for a bit,
He was (so it seemed) in a haze.
So they stood where they were and continued to chat,
Why I think they have been there for days!

"Somewhere is that way" said the Ibis...

YELLA UMBRELLA FELLA

"Holding that yella umbrella, green fella,
You look funny, there's no downpour to come.
There's no cloud around
No thundering sound
So holding that, don't you feel dumb?"

"I'm aware of the sun" said the Green guy,
And I know it won't rain, not today.
but the sun makes me hot,
with this brolly, I'm not,
Plus it's yellow and merry and gay."

30

HORTENSE AND THE FROG

Hortense, an only child, had been taught all through her life,
To be respectful, quite polite and never rude.
She had wished for a companion, a wee bunny or a pup,
or a kitty, not this greenish warty dude.

Grumpy Geoff the Genie was available at times
To grant wishes and desires of young and old.
One had to really want a thing, and feel it in their heart
and have the courage to then ask and be quite bold.

Grumpy Geoff became quite testy as his hair began to thin
and later could not hear what people asked.
So to state to him quite clearly, in a happy bouncy way,
means his job of making magic's less a task.

Hortense chose a starry night, and bravely found her way
to the Genie's home just out beyond the bog.
"Thank you, but I need to return this little guy
'Cause you see, he's not a puppy, he's a Frog."

The Genie huffed and puffed and snorted just a bit,
but Hortense was firm and wasn't to be daunted.
It all took quite a while, But Hortense was so polite
That old Geoffrey finally gave her what she wanted.

SYLVIA'S NEW HAT

Sylvia Waddlesworth had her own style
She wore what she wanted, would travel a mile
if she knew there was fashion ahead.

Sylvia Waddlesworth knew about trends
She read all the magazines right to the ends
to learn what was hot and what wasn't.

Sylvia Waddlesworth loved her big coat
She adored her bag that was too large to tote
so she'd drag it when she went a-walking.

Sylvia Waddlesworth says "it's just fine,
I'll wear what I want when asked out to dine.
I feel good, and that's all that counts".

Sylvia Waddlesworth did up her hair
She combed it and poofed it high up in the air
then she put on her newly bought hat.

Sylvia Waddlesworth felt very smart
She knew that her taste was a matter of art
just ask her, she's one in a million.

Well Sylvia.... it's...ummm....

it's...YOU!°...I think you should keep it.°

...she should
burn it....

SHARING

"Isn't it funny" said giraffe to sunflower

"That I'm all splotchy and you're so bright!

But we're best of friends and we visit a lot,

(but to others we must seem a sight!)".

"That's what's so fun", said sunflower to giraffe

"That's all a part of our game,

When we love what's different about each other,

We're free to learn what's the same".

The Artist

JUDI LIGHT is British born, Canadian raised and, after living abroad and in many cities across the U.S., she now resides in Venice, Florida.

Judi has been a caricature artist for most of her life, creating black and white whimsy pieces which have been published as cards, coloring books and for private collections. She has also dabbled in mixed media and 3D art using various types of clay and acrylics.

She recently revisited her Wee Folk (who were patiently awaiting her return), with the added bonus of discovering the total joy of water colors. And that's when the Magic happened!

She is truly an artist who uses her creativity, realism, passion and artistry to make whimsical, touching, humorous paintings that uplift and lighten the soul.

Using engineering pens in a combination of line and pointilism, then layers of watercolor washes, she creates very luminous color and depth in her paintings, making them seem to glow. As they are packed with detail, take your time enjoying each piece.

Judi says that "... the purpose of my Wee Folk art is to ramp up the 'Happiness Factor, possibly encourage some insight, perhaps impart a life lesson... and ALWAYS to leave you smiling' .

You may write to her at: judi@LightTouchArt.com and purchase limited edition Gyclée prints of her Twigshire characters, plus cards, book-marks and more! at: http://LightTouchArt.com

Comments from our weekly paper "Twigshire Twitterings"

Each time we look at your art, we see something else, something new in each print! The same is true with "Harry Takes 5!" Looking today at Harry on our wall, we see the blissful look on his face, the detail in his shirt, the brillance of the colors, the movement of Harry's body as he "Takes 5!" We just love it! Thank you for entering our world! Your art is peaceful and happy! - Pat Hartung

Thank you for sharing your creative genius with our walls! We love the unique style of your creations; they are truly one-of-a-kind. Much love and hugs. - Carina & Jeff Long

We were gifted with "Sharing" and find it a smile-maker each and every day. The world needs this: More Whimsey. - Duane B.

Looking at a work of art as great as yours put a smile on my face and a feeling of happiness. A great artist brings out the emotions in someone. Thank you. - Scarlett

Your art work is superb indeed! Your talents are by far above and beyond glorious! Continue to create these amazing little friends to share with the world! They are a gift to us all!! - Sulianna Chandler

Harry touched my soul. I work in the Timeshare Industry telling people how important it is to take the time and vacation. I am "Harry" and I am not taking the time to stop and smell the roses. - Chris Dishon

I am in love! You are such a talent! Please don't ever stop sharing your imagination!! - Bayla B.

Seeing all of Judi's delightful work come together in a book was delightful and awe inspiring! I loved seeing the water colour drawings on line but to see them in book format with detailed text is so cool. Kudos to you and Judi for the amount of work that has gone into making this book come to fruition. I can hardly wait to order copies. - Maria Hedderson, Teaching Librarian

(Continued)

"Twigshire Twitterings" continued...

I am in love with Judi's artwork! I purchased a print of Yella Umbrella Fella for my two infant cousins (girls). They were enthralled! I know that they will enjoy having this print in their room for many, many years to come. I surely would have loved having it in my room...it's just sooooooo happy! - Linda Yannuzzi

Your art and talent are absolutely amazing. You products are wonderful. Thank you for being you. - Barbara

I have Manny Baba and Odette in my home. It's the first thing I look at when coming in. I really enjoy Judi's work. It always makes me smile. - Tammy Graham

The picture of Fiona is fun and quirky. When I look at it I smile, feel happy and Cheerful. - Bailee Frere

In the Twigshire book Ms. Light weaves life lessons for children (and reminders for adults) to show kindness and love toward others, to live life fully, and to treat and respect yourself well. Colorful, detailed paintings of fascinating whimsical characters accompany each narrative. As a parent, grandparent, and retired elementary teacher I see great value in this book as a spark for many discussions in the home and in the classroom. I bought the book to share with visiting grandchildren and I'm recommending it to my former fellow teachers. - Terry L.

I love the whimsical, fun figures and stories. I am fascinated by your drawing technique and the time and patience to produce a picture. Finally finishing it with bright, clear watercolours. WOW!! Each time I look at "Flying High" I am reminded that no matter what Life challenges we have, we always have a choice to be happy. When I first saw "Cedric" I just knew I had to buy it for my daughter's birthday. You see, my daughter, her husband and son are all "short stature". "Stools" are an every day part of their life. On a stool, they ARE TALL and can do ANYTHING!! I love the expressions and the vibrant colours. You are not only talented, but have an amazing heart! - Judy Remple

READER REVIEWS FROM AMAZON.COM

CAPTIVATING! - by Amelia Curzon Reviews

The Magical World of Twigshire is a collection of vignettes revolving around the enchanting occupants of Twigshire village. We meet such characters as Hortense, Emelda Flapjacket, Mr Bumberdorn and Scrum and Angelo, as they go about their daily lives doing wonderful things. We can even learn how to make `Limp Imp Soup'. That was one of my favourites. It seems, after you have made your soup, you can dry out the imps, the main ingredient, and re-use them time and time again, and...they don't mind a bit.

Gifted author and artist Judi Light has created a work filled with whimsical and entrancing illustrations, which are really more like lovable caricatures, and which I personally found reminiscent of the great (late) satirical cartoonist Ronald Searle. Ms Light's illustrations are glorious; vibrant, highly detailed and so beautifully drawn that you can look at them forever and still keep seeing more. In fact, the whole book is absolutely charming; loaded with touches of magic and sweet little messages about feeling good inside. Beautifully written in a mixture of text and poetry, the reader is transported into a captivating world of happiness, kindness and the enjoyment of life. There is just so much for young children to enjoy (and adults too) and so many lessons for them to learn. Utter magic!

LOTS OF HAPPINESS - by Denver Sky, Author

The illustrations are charming, and the stories behind them add to the smiles. The whimsical Twigshire characters impart life lessons and gentle insights which make it a perfect gift for children or adults. I bought it as Christmas present for a best friend, but it would also make a terrific get-well-soon gift for a relative who's under the weather. In Twigshire, the weather is unusually magical!

Real Art Made Accessible - by WhimseyJess

I received the Magical World of Twigshire as a gift for me and my 20 month old baby and it is a phenomenon. I'm giving it as a holiday gift to all of my friends with kids! Charlie and I love books where the art is great and the story is compelling and well-written! Light's illustrations in this book are bright, colorful, energetic and fun - and really engaging for the little guy! Light is an amazing artist and she (like Beatrix Potter, Maurice Sendak, Dr. Seuss and others before her) makes real art accessible to everyone. I love to introduce Charlie to these and other artists. He loves to point to the Twigshire characters and make their sounds (what does a turtle say?)! I'm not sure that his language is developed enough to really appreciate the content of the fantastic stories that go along with each illustration but I know that they are a great way to start a conversation about what we value (kindness, generosity, acceptance) and the babe loves the fun rhymes! This is, as advertised, a feel good book for all ages!

Pure Delight, Warm Your Heart, Beautiful Magical Stories - by Suliana

From the first page to the last, this book will warm your heart. You will get lost in your imagination as you become part of this magical world and enjoy each and every story the Twigshire folks have to tell. The paintings are just exquisite, the characters are unlike any others you have ever seen. I just fell in love with Fiona, Hortense and Sylvia. The details are amazing and the colors so bright and vibrant! This is a perfect book for anyone you LOVE, child, teen or adult. I am looking forward to the next book all ready! I would highly recommend this book to ALL!

A Great Book For Home and School - by Terry L.

In the Twigshire book Ms. Light weaves life lessons for children (and reminders for adults) to show kindness and love toward others, to live life fully, and to treat and respect yourself well. Colorful, detailed paintings of fascinating whimsical characters accompany each narrative. As a parent, grandparent, and retired elementary teacher I see great value in this book as a spark for many discussions in the home and in the classroom. I bought the book to share with visiting grandchildren and I'm recommending it to my former fellow teachers.

Familiar Friend - by Eileen B.

When I first saw the cover of Vol. 1 about Twigshire, I felt like I was looking at a familiar friend . . . and as I entered the wonderful world of Twigshire, I felt like I'd already met some of the others, too! I can't wait for Vol. 2 to come out! I've introduced my oldest daughter & soon will introduce my granddaughters to my Twigshire friends.

A Real Joy - by Sari M.

Between the verse and the illustrations, I was brought into another world -- the world of Poom and his wonderful hamlet Twigshire, and all the characters who live there. Judi, your artwork is astounding .... the detail and colors so clear and bright. Thank you for allowing me the pleasure to visit; I smiled all the way through.

Why Should Kids Have All The Fun? - by Burt K., Writer

At first glance, it would be easy to classify Judi Light's delightful The Magical World of Twigshire" as catnip for the kindergarten set. That would be a serious miscalculation. The wonderful illustrations and sparkling prose have literal worlds to offer kids and adults alike. This is not so much whimsy as wit -- frequently laugh out loud wit. The drawings of fantastical creatures beg for repeated viewings, and provide new rewards every time. By all means, read Ms. Light's book to the children, but prepare to be enchanted yourself. And don't be surprised to find yourself yearning to be in Frog Swallow Lake for a Fish Mist Facial at Zelda's Hot Spot Spa. Highly recommended.